GOLD LEAF BOOKS

## Tor Mark Press

Thanks are due for the expertise and knowledge of
Matthew Stevens of M Stevens & Son, fishmongers of St Ives

First published 2010, 2015
This edition 2018

ISBN 978 0 85025 439 6 Cornwall
ISBN 978 0 85025 441 9 Devon

Published by Tor Mark,
United Downs Industrial Estate,
St Day, Redruth, Cornwall TR16 5HY

www.tormark.co.uk

Printed by Booths Print,
The Praze, Penryn, Cornwall TR10 8AA

# FISH
# RECIPES

Heather Corbett

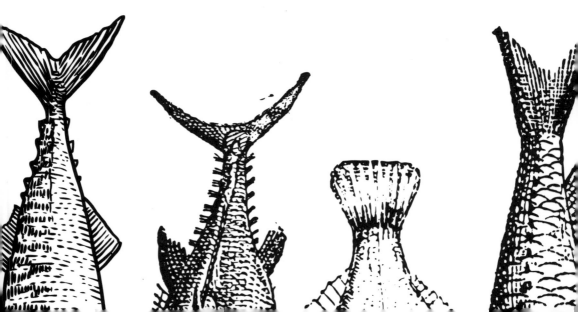

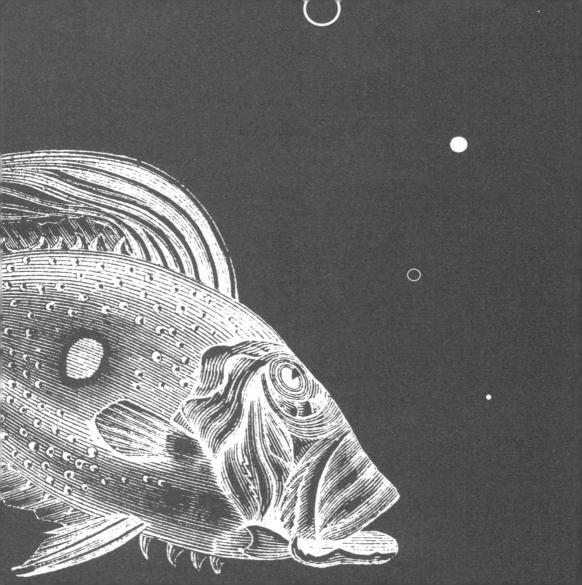

# CONTENTS

| | |
|---|---|
| INTRODUCTION | 7 |
| COD WITH CORIANDER & SAFFRON | 10 |
| COD WITH RUNNER BEANS | 11 |
| COD WITH CUCUMBER, SPRING ONIONS & CREAM | 12 |
| FISH CRUMBLE | 14 |
| RED GURNARD FILLETS WITH CELERY & APPLE | 16 |
| SMOKED HADDOCK & MUSHROOM LASAGNE | 17 |
| SMOKED HADDOCK & SPINACH TART | 19 |
| SPANISH HAKE | 21 |
| HAKE STEAKS WITH LEMON & GREEN OLIVES | 22 |
| PEPPERED HERRING | 23 |
| RED FILLETS OF JOHN DORY | 24 |
| SILVER MULLET WITH ROASTED VEGETABLES | 26 |
| WHITE FISH WITH BRIE | 29 |
| BAKED MACKEREL WITH CIDER, ORANGE & CHIVES | 30 |
| SMOKED MACKEREL INSTANT PASTA | 31 |
| SMOKED MACKEREL, POTATOES & LEEKS | 33 |

MONKFISH RISOTTO WITH SAFFRON 36

MONKFISH & BACON 38

WEST COUNTRY PLAICE 39

PLAICE WITH GARLIC MUSHROOMS 40

POLLACK WITH MAYONNAISE & YOGHURT 42

SARDINE WITH MUSTARD & CIDER 43

STUFFED SARDINES 44

SCALLOPS WITH LEEKS & CORIANDER 45

RED, WHITE & GREEN SCALLOPS 46

SEA BASS WITH FRESH HERB BUTTER 47

SEAFOOD WITH MUSTARD & CREAM 48

MEGRIM SOLE WITH CLOTTED CREAM & CHIVES 50

TORBAY SOLE STUFFED WITH CRAB & PRAWNS 51

SQUID WITH GARLIC, CORIANDER & OLIVES 53

HOT SQUID SALAD 55

TUNA AND CORIANDER, LEMON & WHITE WINE 57

TUNA STEW 58

GREEK HADDOCK 60

# AN INTRODUCTION

Fish is the original fast food – in earlier times cooked quickly over a fire or baked in the embers. Fish is good for you! It does not have the calories of meat, yet it has a similar vitamin content. Oily fish like mackerel, herring and sardines have the added bonus of reducing the possibility of heart disease and strokes.

These recipes are easy, fast, successful and interesting. I have cooked – and adapted them – over the years for family and friends. Fish cookery is far more enticing and exciting than it used to be. Forget those childhood memories of fishy smells and a mouthful of bones – fish cooking has grown up and is the ultimate quality food in this busy world. Many of the recipes in this book are interchangeable – if you haven't got all the ingredients, be confident, substitute. Above all, be inventive and enjoy the results! Nearly all these recipes are cooked in a hot oven, giving a double advantage – the lack of smell and the fish is cooked very fast in one dish. Once it's in the oven you just have time for a sip of wine and voilà your dinner is ready!

The fish used in these recipes are those caught all around the coast of the South-west and sold at the fish markets of Newlyn, Padstow, Looe, Plymouth and Brixham. Much from these markets goes 'up country' or, sadly, is exported to Europe – Spain and France buy a good deal of British fish and in both countries restaurants around the coast have a reputation for cooking 'local' fish! Newlyn has the second largest fishing fleet in Britain. You can walk along the quay, look at the fishing boats and see the fish market. Most of the boats are beam trawlers. They have a crew of five and fish up to 100 miles out, in winds often reaching gale force, for a week at a time before returning home for a few days.

Fish caught in the West Country are available throughout Britain in local fishmongers and at supermarket fish stalls. Whenever possible buy fish that is fresh, rather than frozen, and cook it quickly – that way the fish will have the best possible taste. Shop with an open mind – go for what looks good on the day.

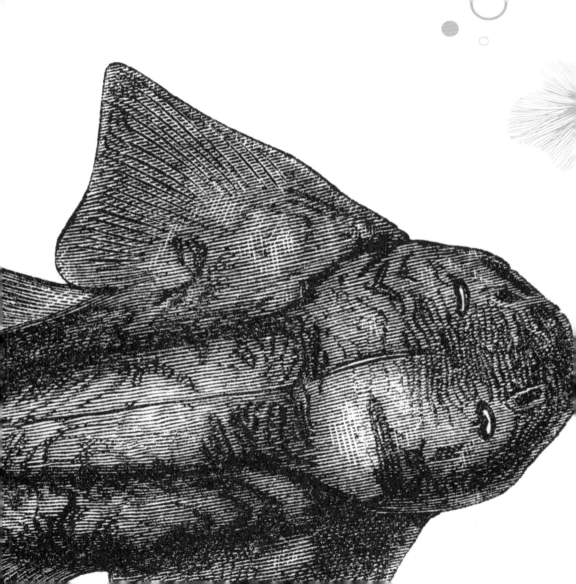

# COD WITH CORIANDER & SAFFRON

*Serves 4*

This is an unusual use of cod, which makes a change from many other recipes, and is a very pretty dish. When cod is not available this dish would work well with silver mullet or pollack.

## INGREDIENTS

4 x 150g/5 oz pieces of cod fillet

1 teaspoon crushed green peppercorns

1 teaspoon crushed coriander seeds

12 strands of saffron

225ml/8 fl oz white wine

110ml/4 fl oz olive oil

12 cherry tomatoes

1 tablespoon chopped parsley

1 tablespoon balsamic vinegar

Bring the white wine to the boil and pour over the roughly chopped green peppercorns, coriander seeds and saffron. Pour a little of the olive oil into an ovenproof dish, lay in the 4 pieces of cod and the cherry tomatoes. Cover with the saffron and white wine mix, and add a little more olive oil.

Cook in a hot oven 230ºC/450ºF/gas mark 8 for about 15 minutes. Before serving, add the balsamic vinegar and the parsley. Serve with plain rice or couscous.

# COD WITH RUNNER BEANS

*Serves 4*

This is a surprising and wonderful dish based on a Jamie Oliver recipe that I found in a newspaper. The runner beans could be replaced by French beans.

## INGREDIENTS

4 x 110-175 g/4-6 oz pieces of cod fillet

4 slices smoked bacon

450 g/1 lb runner beans thinly sliced

12 cherry tomatoes

12 black olives

olive oil

2 lemons halved

1 tablespoon chopped parsley or chives

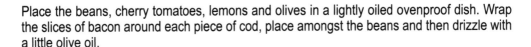

Place the beans, cherry tomatoes, lemons and olives in a lightly oiled ovenproof dish. Wrap the slices of bacon around each piece of cod, place amongst the beans and then drizzle with a little olive oil.

Cook in a hot oven 230°C/450°F/gas mark 8 for about 15 minutes, depending on the size of the cod. Decorate with the chopped parsley or chives. This dish goes well with plain rice or couscous.

# COD WITH CUCUMBER, SPRING ONIONS & CREAM

*Serves 4*

Cooked cucumber may seem odd but it adds a wonderful colour and texture to the dish. Cod is more readily available than it used to be; I'm told that there are always plenty two miles off Newlyn in the spring.

## INGREDIENTS

450 g/1 lb cod fillets cut into large pieces

4 spring onions finely chopped

10 cm/4 inches cucumber roughly chopped

olive oil

1 glass white wine

200 ml/7 fl oz double cream

$\frac{1}{2}$ tablespoon chopped dill or parsley

Drizzle a little olive oil onto the base of an ovenproof dish and place the cod fillets on top. Place the spring onions and cucumber on top of the fish and then add the white wine.

Bake in a hot oven 230ºC/450ºF/gas mark 8 for about 15 minutes, depending on the thickness of the fish. Add the cream and the dill or parsley, and return to the oven to heat through. This dish is good with new potatoes and French beans.

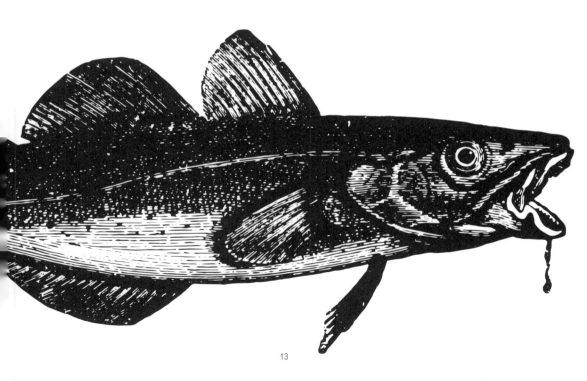

# FISH CRUMBLE

*Serves 4*

Any fish will do for this homely dish, although it's nice to get a range of textures – a little cooked salmon adds a lovely colour as well as texture and flavour.

## INGREDIENTS

450 g/1 lb assorted white fish (see above)

20 cooked prawns (defrosted if using frozen)

2 hard boiled eggs roughly chopped

1 tablespoon chopped parsley

4 spring onions chopped

*For the crumble:*

40 g/1½ oz butter

75 g/3 oz plain flour

50 g/2 oz Cheddar cheese grated

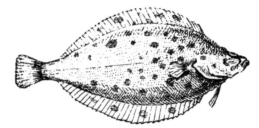

*For the sauce:*

40 g/1½ oz butter

40 g/1½ oz plain flour

250 ml/8 fl oz milk

125 ml/4 fl oz cider or white wine

coarse sea salt and ground black pepper to taste

Make the crumble by rubbing the butter into the flour to form breadcrumbs and then adding the cheese. Make the sauce, by melting the butter in a saucepan before mixing in the flour and allowing the two to cook for a moment. Add the milk and the cider or wine very slowly indeed – being too enthusiastic here will cause the sauce to go lumpy. Season with salt and pepper to taste.

Place all the fish, prawns, egg, parsley and spring onions into an ovenproof dish and pour the sauce over. Top with the crumble mix and cook in a hot oven 230°C/450°F/gas mark 8 for 15-20 minutes until cooked through.

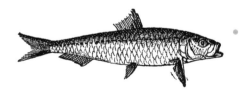

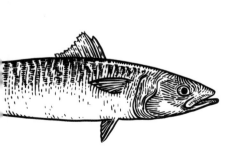

# RED GURNARD FILLETS
# WITH CELERY & APPLE

*Serves 4*

Gurnard needs to be well filleted, as small pinbones left in can be very irksome. It has a good flavour and is quite firm. The skin is a beautiful pinky red which looks very pretty peeping through the sauce. It is available all the year round.

## INGREDIENTS

4 red gurnard filleted

3 sticks of celery sliced thinly

2 apples chopped into small chunks

4 spring onions chopped

25g/1oz butter

275ml/10 fl oz single cream

1 tablespoon French flat leaf parsley chopped

1 tablespoon chopped walnuts for decoration

Butter an ovenproof dish. Place the gurnard fillets in it, and sprinkle the celery, apple and spring onions on top. Pour over the single cream, cover with tinfoil and put in a hot oven 230ºC/450ºF/gas mark 8.

Cook for 10 minutes, uncover and cook for a further 5 minutes. Decorate with the parsley and the walnuts. Serve with broccoli and mashed potatoes sprinkled with some more French parsley.

# SMOKED HADDOCK
# & MUSHROOM LASAGNE

*Serves 4*

Surprisingly, fish makes good lasagne – shellfish can also be used successfully.

## INGREDIENTS

450 g/1 lb smoked haddock fillets, cooked and flaked

1 onion roughly chopped

110 g/4 oz mushrooms chopped

1 x 400 g/14 oz tin chopped tomatoes

paprika

coarse sea salt and ground black pepper to taste

1 tablespoon chopped parsley

olive oil

9 sheets egg lasagne – the sort that does not require pre-cooking

275 ml/10 fl oz plain yoghurt

1 egg

4 tablespoons grated Parmesan

Fry the onion and the mushrooms in a little oil to soften. Add the tomatoes, a large pinch of paprika, sea salt and ground black pepper to taste. Cook for 5 minutes.

In an oiled ovenproof dish place a third of the smoked haddock, then a third of the tomato sauce mixture. Place 3 sheets of lasagne on top. Repeat twice more.

Mix the yoghurt, egg and 3 tablespoons Parmesan together and spread over the last layer of lasagne. Sprinkle the remaining Parmesan on top. Bake in a medium oven 180ºC/350ºF/gas mark 4 for 25 minutes or until cooked. Decorate with parsley.

# SMOKED HADDOCK & SPINACH TART

*Serves 4*

Smoked fish and spinach seem to be natural companions and in a tart the mix of colours is delightful.

## INGREDIENTS

*For the pastry:*

110 g/4 oz plain flour

50 g/2 oz butter

water to mix


*For the filling:*

450 g/1 lb spinach cooked, well drained and chopped

225 g/8 oz smoked haddock, cooked and flaked

2 tomatoes

3 eggs

275 ml/10 fl oz milk

150 ml/5 fl oz double cream

1 tablespoon grated Parmesan

1 tablespoon parsley chopped

coarse sea salt and ground black pepper

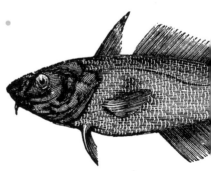

Make the pastry in the usual way, rubbing the fat into the flour and adding the water to mix – place in the fridge to keep cool. Whisk the eggs with the milk, cream and the parsley, and season to taste with coarse sea salt and ground black pepper.

Roll out the pastry and place in a 20 cm/8 inch flan dish. Add the spinach and the haddock, and pour over the egg mix to cover. Slice the tomatoes and arrange decoratively on top, and sprinkle with Parmesan. Bake at 180ºC/350ºF/gas mark 4 for 35-40 minutes until cooked.

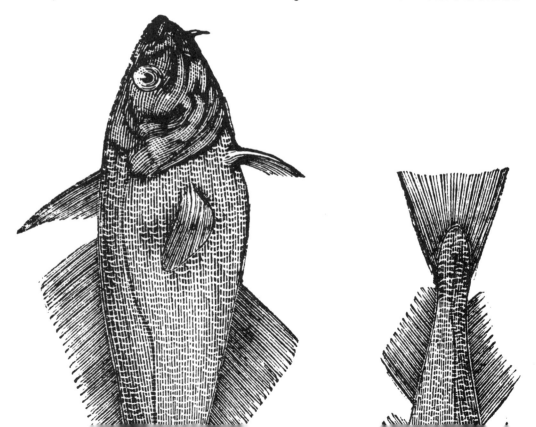

# SPANISH HAKE

*Serves 4*

Much of the hake caught in our waters is exported to Spain, where it is highly valued. If you are lucky enough to find some hake in your fishmonger's, do not hesitate to buy it – it has enough character to be combined with strong Mediterranean flavours. This recipe is based on one found in Spain on holiday. It was so good, I had to bring it home!

## INGREDIENTS

4 x 110 g/4 oz pieces of hake

50 g/2 oz chorizo sausage chopped into small cubes

1 large onion chopped

2 medium courgettes sliced thinly

1 x 400 g/14 oz tin chopped tomatoes

olive oil

150 ml/5 fl oz sherry

¼ teaspoon paprika

1 lemon sliced into wedges

sea salt and ground black pepper to taste

First fry the chopped onion and the chorizo together. When softened, place in the bottom of an ovenproof dish. Add the 4 pieces of hake, and cover them with the thin slices of courgette and the paprika. Mix the chopped tomato and the sherry, add a little salt and pepper, and pour over the assembled ingredients.

Place in a hot oven 230°C/450°F/gas mark 8 for 20 minutes. Serve with plain boiled rice and lemon wedges.

# HAKE STEAKS WITH LEMON & GREEN OLIVES

*Serves 4*

If hake is difficult to find, then cod is a good substitute.

## INGREDIENTS

4 x 110 g/4 oz hake steaks

juice of 1 lemon

2 tablespoons olive oil and a little more

1 tablespoon chopped parsley

2 cloves garlic chopped

4 tablespoons breadcrumbs

coarse sea salt and ground black pepper

12 green olives pitted and roughly chopped

First marinate the hake steaks in the lemon juice and olive oil for at least an hour – but longer is better, if you can remember. Mix the breadcrumbs, parsley, salt, pepper and garlic.

Place the fish in an ovenproof dish with the marinade – sprinkle the breadcrumb topping over the fish and place in a hot oven 230ºC/450ºF/gas mark 8 for 20 minutes. Decorate with the olives before serving. Rice goes well with this dish.

# PEPPERED HERRING

Herring is around for much of the year, is readily available and is reasonably versatile. It has quite a strong flavour and a creamy texture. One of the most successful recipes is herring dipped in oatmeal – here is an interesting variation.

## INGREDIENTS

4 herrings filleted

olive oil

1 tablespoon black peppercorns

1 tablespoon flour

balsamic vinegar (if liked)

Crush the black peppercorns in a mortar and pestle or in a polythene bag with a rolling pin, mix with the flour and spread out on a large plate. Roll the herrings on both sides in the mixture and place in an oiled ovenproof dish. Sprinkle a little olive oil over the top and bake in a hot oven 230°C/450°F/gas mark 8 for 10 minutes.

Serve with a very little balsamic vinegar sprinkled on top. A robust red wine, French bread and French beans are excellent with this dish.

# RED FILLETS OF JOHN DORY

*Serves 4*

John Dory is an unusual fish with a good texture which flakes slightly when cut with a knife. It is firm so that the fillets hold their shape when cooked and is available for much of the year.

## INGREDIENTS

2 John Dory filleted

16 cherry tomatoes

1 red pepper thinly sliced

olive oil

juice of half a lemon

4 spring onions finely chopped

$\frac{1}{2}$ tablespoon chopped parsley

small pinch of paprika

Pour a small quantity of olive oil in an ovenproof dish, and place the John Dory fillets, cut in half lengthways for easier serving, on top.

Add the red pepper, cherry tomatoes, lemon juice and paprika, cover with tin foil and place in a hot oven 230°C/450°F/gas mark 8 for about 15 minutes. Uncover and add the spring onions and parsley.

This is very good served with a small quantity of mushroom and herb risotto.

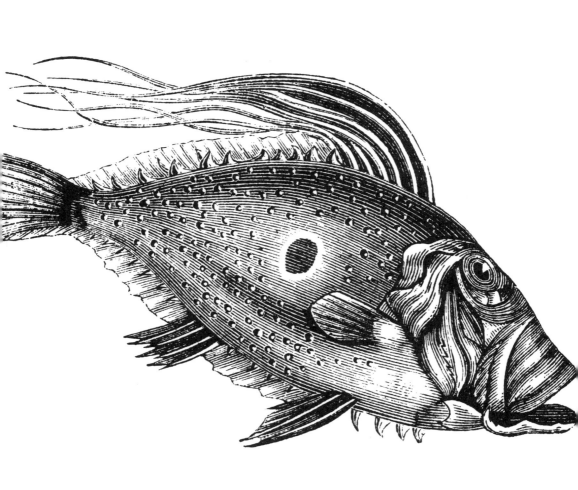

# SILVER MULLET WITH
# ROASTED VEGETABLES

*Serves 4*

Although the name silver mullet does not sound very enticing, it is a fine fish – quite firm and robust. They can be a good size so that one fish between two may be ample, you will need to decide this yourself.

## INGREDIENTS

2 silver mullet filleted

1 red pepper cut into chunks

2 medium courgettes chopped roughly

2 small red onions roughly chopped

2 sprigs of thyme

1 ripe avocado chopped into small cubes

275 ml/10 fl oz natural yoghurt

¼ teaspoon paprika

3 tablespoons olive oil

coarse sea salt and ground black pepper

Place the vegetables in an ovenproof dish with 2 tablespoons of the olive oil. Add the sprigs of thyme and a little salt and pepper. Roast in a hot oven 230°C/450°F/gas mark 8 for 20 minutes. Remove from the oven; place the silver mullet fillets on top, flesh side up. Drizzle the remainder of the olive oil over the fish and return to the oven for a further 10 minutes or until the fish is cooked.

While the fish is cooking, make the avocado raita by combining the yoghurt and the chopped avocado. Sprinkle a little paprika on the top as decoration. This raita should be offered with the fish, rather than being poured over it. New potatoes go well with this dish.

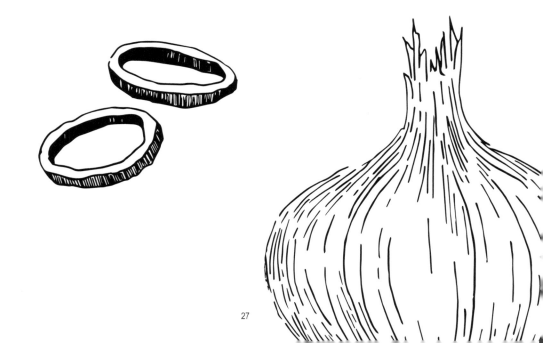

# WHITE FISH WITH BRIE

*Serves 4*

This is a very useful way of using up any left over cooked white fish – cod, pollack, mullet, monkfish, plaice, sole... anything will be fine. The recipe is so good it is worth cooking fish especially for it – simply bring the fish to the boil in a saucepan and then leave to cool. Sorry, this will make a fishy smell, so open the window or close the kitchen door!

## INGREDIENTS

450 g/1 lb cooked white fish

175 g/6 oz mushrooms thinly sliced

2 cloves of garlic crushed

2 tablespoons chopped chives and/or parsley

ground black pepper

225 g/8 oz Brie

butter

Flake the cooked fish into bite-sized chunks. Butter an ovenproof serving dish and place the fish in one layer. The finely sliced mushrooms are placed on top of this with a little ground black pepper, 1 tablespoon of the herbs and the crushed garlic. Finally add a layer of Brie, which has been cut into 6 mm/$\frac{1}{4}$ inch slices – do not cut off the rind, as it gives an interesting chewy texture.

Place in a hot oven 230°C/450°F/gas mark 8 for 15 minutes when the Brie should be wonderfully runny. Decorate with the remainder of the chopped herbs. New potatoes and peas or French beans go nicely with this dish.

# BAKED MACKEREL WITH CIDER, ORANGE & CHIVES

*Serves 4*

Fresh mackerel is a beautiful fish to look at – silver and blue green. It is essential that it is eaten as fresh as possible – it does not keep well: this is why so much is smoked (the best mackerel for smoking are those caught during the winter months from November to March, as they are much more oily). Increasingly mackerel in the South-west are line caught – these are the ones you should buy to ensure that mackerel fishing is sustainable. The orange in this recipe offsets the oiliness of the fish.

## INGREDIENTS

4 mackerel fillets

150 ml/5 fl oz cider

2 oranges

4 spring onions chopped

olive oil

coarse sea salt and ground black pepper

Grate the orange rind, peel the oranges and cut into slices. Place half the orange slices on the base of an ovenproof dish, arrange the mackerel fillets on top, place the remainder of the orange slices over the fish, and then sprinkle the orange rind and the spring onion on top. Pour the cider over the fish and season to taste.

Put in a hot oven 230°C/450°F/gas mark 8 for 10-15 minutes until cooked. Serve with French bread and a salad.

# SMOKED MACKEREL INSTANT PASTA

*Serves 4*

In Cornwall and Devon there are a number of small firms smoking not only mackerel, haddock and cod but all sorts of fish and meats. Smoked mackerel adds a distinctive flavour to old favourites, such as cauliflower cheese or macaroni cheese. Simply flake the smoked mackerel fillets and add to the cheese sauce.

## INGREDIENTS

4 smoked mackerel fillets flaked

450 g/1 lb fresh pasta

570 ml/1 pt single cream

1 tablespoon grated Parmesan

4 spring onions roughly chopped

225 g/8 oz mushrooms roughly chopped butter

salt and ground black pepper to taste

1 tablespoon chopped parsley

Gently cook the mushrooms and spring onions in the melted butter in a saucepan for 5 minutes over a medium heat until softened. Add the flaked smoked mackerel and heat through, and then add the cream, making sure that you do not allow it to boil.

Cook the fresh pasta as directed on the packet, place in a serving dish, add the mackerel, mushrooms, spring onions and the grated Parmesan, and mix together lightly. Sprinkle with the chopped parsley and ground black pepper to taste.

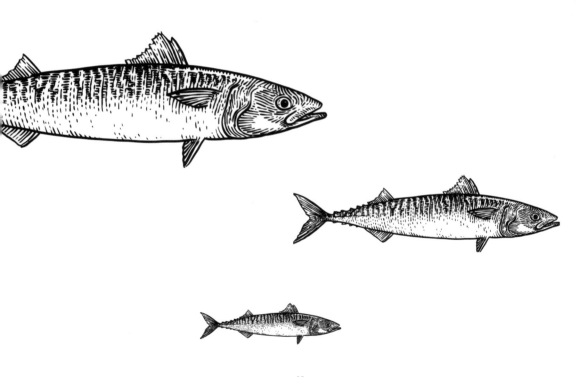

# SMOKED MACKEREL, POTATOES & LEEKS

*Serves 4*

Smoked mackerel is a useful store cupboard fish, as it keeps for some time vacuum-packed in the fridge or even longer in the freezer. This is a truly classic dish and can be varied in a number of ways very effectively.

## INGREDIENTS

4 small smoked mackerel fillets

2 medium leeks cut across into 5mm/$\frac{1}{4}$in slices

275ml/10floz single cream

200ml/7floz milk

1 tablespoon grain mustard or horseradish sauce

450g/1lb potatoes, peeled and cut into 5mm/$\frac{1}{4}$in slices

butter

salt and ground black pepper to taste


Butter an ovenproof dish. Place in it a layer of potatoes, then leeks, then flaked smoked mackerel. Repeat this and finish with a layer of potato.

Mix together the cream, milk and mustard or horseradish. Carefully pour this over the top so that it goes through the layers, adding ground black pepper to taste. Cover with tin foil and put in a hot oven 230°C/450°F/gas mark 8 for about 50 minutes.

Test the middle of the dish with a skewer to see if the potato is cooked – when this is the case, remove the tin foil and cook for another 10 minutes to brown the potatoes on top.

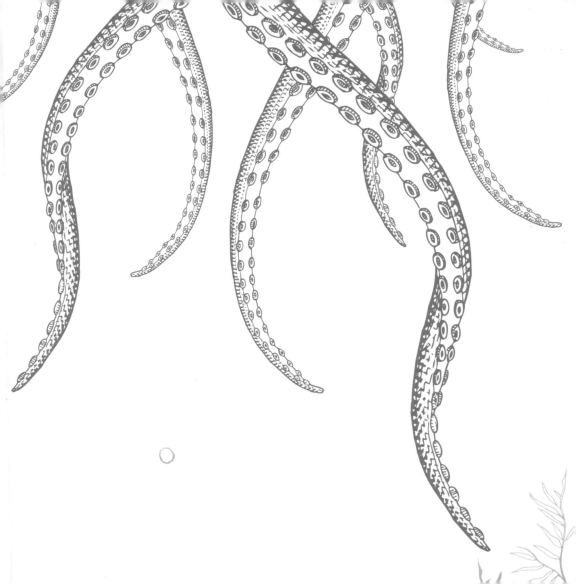

# MONKFISH RISOTTO WITH SAFFRON

*Serves 4*

Monkfish, tuna, shellfish and squid all lend themselves to being made into risotto.

## INGREDIENTS

450 g/1 lb monkfish fillet cut into bite-size chunks

1 onion chopped

2 green peppers chopped

2 cloves garlic crushed

12 saffron threads

½ teaspoon paprika

225 g/8 oz Arborio risotto rice

1 glass white wine, vermouth or sherry

425 ml/15 fl oz fish or vegetable stock

1 tablespoon French parsley chopped

a few (defrosted) cooked prawns for decoration

lemon wedges

coarse sea salt and ground black pepper to taste

olive oil

Fry the monkfish pieces in oil in a large frying or paella pan until they are nearly cooked. Remove and set aside. Fry the onion, garlic and the peppers gently until soft, then add the rice, stirring so that all the grains are covered with oil. Cover with the hot stock in which you have infused the saffron, and add the wine, vermouth or sherry, paprika and salt and pepper. Leave on a medium heat to cook – do not stir.

After 10 minutes return the monkfish to the pan, pushing it into and amongst the rice. Continue to simmer until the rice is cooked and the liquid more or less evaporated. If the rice is not cooked but is dry, add a little more liquid – water or wine – and continue to cook.

Decorate with prawns, lemon wedges and parsley.

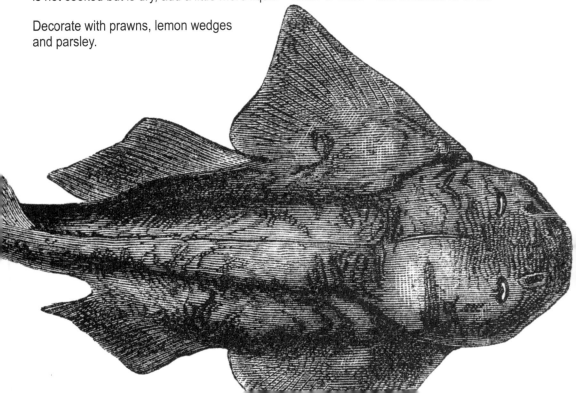

# MONKFISH & BACON

*Serves 4*

This is a traditional French recipe which is always a surprise when brought to the table. Monkfish is a versatile fish, as it can be used in a number of ways – either in large pieces which are 'carved' as here or in smaller pieces for a risotto. It is available all year round. The recipes for tuna stew or squid with garlic, coriander and olives would do very well with monkfish.

## INGREDIENTS

700 g/1½ lb monkfish tail in a piece

4-6 rashers of smoked bacon

8 sage leaves

2 cloves garlic crushed

olive oil

balsamic vinegar or lemon juice

Firstly make sure that the fishmonger has taken the central bone out of the monkfish and cleaned off all the skin. The fish should still be more or less in one piece.

Arrange the sage leaves and the garlic along the length of the fish and then wrap the bacon rashers around it. Put in an oiled roasting pan and drizzle a little olive oil over it. Place in a hot oven 230°C/450°F/gas mark 8 for 30 minutes.

Remove the fish to a serving dish and drizzle a little balsamic vinegar or lemon juice over. The fish should be served in slices about 4 cm/1½ inch thick. This dish would be very good with thickly cut sauté potatoes and a green salad.

# WEST COUNTRY PLAICE

*Serves 4*

Plaice is a succulent, delicate fish, so it is important not to overwhelm it with strong flavoured ingredients. The addition of cider and Cheddar cheese gives a West Country interest while the tomato adds colour. Plaice is at its best from May to December.

## INGREDIENTS

225 g/8 oz chopped onion or leeks (which are prettier)

4 plaice fillets

2 tomatoes thinly sliced

150 ml/5 fl oz dry cider

50 g/2 oz Cheddar cheese grated

butter

1 tablespoon dill chopped

sea salt and ground black pepper to taste

Fry the onion or leek in butter until softened and then put in an ovenproof dish. Add the four plaice fillets on the onion/leek, and put the sliced tomato on top. Sprinkle the cheese and most of the dill over the fish, add sea salt and ground black pepper to taste, and drizzle the cider into the dish.

Place in a hot oven 230ºC/450ºF/gas mark 8 for about 10 minutes before serving. Decorate with the remaining dill.

# PLAICE WITH GARLIC MUSHROOMS

*Serves 4*

Garlic mushrooms are a very popular starter. Here they make plaice into a luscious main course.

## INGREDIENTS

4 small or 2 large plaice filleted

4 cloves garlic chopped

225 g/8 oz mushrooms finely chopped

50 g/2 oz butter

1 tablespoon parsley finely chopped

150 ml/5 fl oz white wine

1 lemon cut into curls or wedges

sea salt and ground black pepper to taste

Soften the butter and beat into it the chopped garlic, parsley and mushrooms. If the plaice are large, cut the fillets in half lengthways. Pour a little of the white wine into an ovenproof dish, place half the fillets on top, spread the mushroom mixture over them and then place the other fillets on top, making a kind of sandwich. Add sea salt and ground black pepper to taste. Cover with the remainder of the wine.

Put in a hot oven 230°C/450°F/gas mark 8 for 15-20 minutes depending on the thickness of the plaice – check after 15 to be on the safe side. Decorate with the lemon which takes away some of the richness of the buttery sauce.

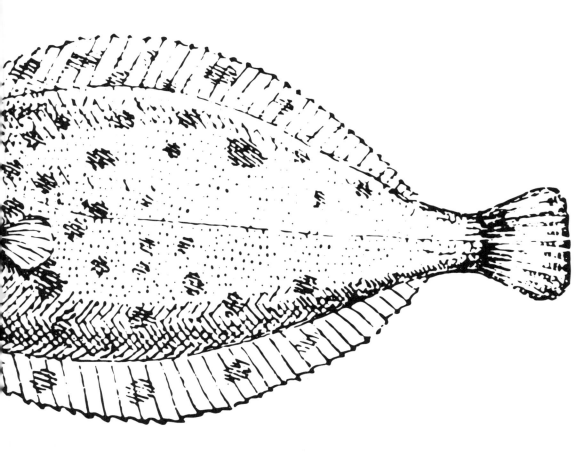

# POLLACK WITH MAYONNAISE & YOGHURT

*Serves 4*

For years pollack has been ignored as a cheap fish and so much of it is exported to Brittany, but now that cod is expensive and less readily available it is coming into its own. The fillets are usually a good size and therefore can be cut into customised portions. It is best from August to March. Mayonnaise and yoghurt seems an odd combination but it makes a very satisfying sauce.

## INGREDIENTS

4 portions of pollack fillet

4 spring onions chopped

4 tablespoons mayonnaise

4 tablespoons plain yoghurt

4 tablespoons breadcrumbs

butter

$\frac{1}{4}$ teaspoon paprika

$\frac{1}{2}$ glass white wine for marinade

First marinate the fillets in the wine for 3-4 hours. Then place the fillets in a buttered ovenproof dish with the marinade, and cover with the mayonnaise and yoghurt previously mixed together. Top with the breadcrumbs mixed with the chopped spring onions.

Place in a hot oven 230ºC/450ºF/gas mark 8 for 15 minutes and serve decorated with a sprinkling of paprika.

# SARDINES WITH MUSTARD & CIDER

*Serves 4*

Sardines are in fact young pilchards and are caught off the Devon and Cornwall coasts in late summer. It is wonderful to see such shiny fresh fish. Sardines, as we prefer to call them (pilchards for us are tinned in tomato sauce), hardly need any preparation at all, simply gutting. If you can't cope with the bones, get them de-boned but remaining in one piece. You may also find them ready prepared in your local supermarket. They are excellent simply grilled on the barbecue, but they can also be cooked in more exotic ways.

## INGREDIENTS

12 de-boned sardines

3 tablespoons coarse grained mustard

olive oil

225 ml/8 fl oz cider

Place the sardines in an oiled ovenproof dish.

Smear each one outside and inside with the mustard and then pour enough cider into the dish to come halfway up the sardines. Bake in a hot oven 230°C/450°F/gas mark 8 for 10 minutes. You may need to top up the cider halfway through the cooking time.

Serve with new potatoes and a green vegetable such as courgettes or spinach.

# STUFFED SARDINES

*Serves 4*

Sardines are such a versatile fish, full of flavour. They are caught in the South-west during the summer when they are plentiful and cheap. Once de-headed, gutted and de-boned, but still remaining in one piece, they lend themselves very well to stuffing. Almost anything will taste good – be inventive!

## INGREDIENTS

12 sardines de-boned

*For mushroom stuffing:*

6 salted sardine fillets or anchovies roughly chopped

110 g/4 oz mushrooms roughly chopped

1 small onion roughly chopped

1 teaspoon dried oregano

1 tablespoon tomato purée

olive oil

ground black pepper to taste

*For red pepper stuffing:*

1 small red onion roughly chopped

1 red pepper roughly chopped

1 tablespoon pine nuts

1 tablespoon sultanas

1 tablespoon tomato purée

1 tablespoon French parsley roughly chopped

olive oil

ground black pepper to taste

Fry the onion and the mushrooms in a little olive oil until softened. Add the remainder of the ingredients, mix and then stuff the sardines. Place in an ovenproof dish and bake in a hot oven 230°C/450°F/gas mark 8 for 10 minutes. Serve with lemon quarters and salad. For red pepper stuffing cook and serve in the same way.

# SCALLOPS WITH LEEKS & CORIANDER

*Serves 4*

Scallops are at their best from December to March. Although 24 scallops will be quite expensive, the superb flavour is not diluted by adding other tastes to pad it out. There is no waste and the dish is prepared and cooked in less than 10 minutes. Halve the ingredients to make an elegant starter.

## INGREDIENTS

24 scallops, cleaned and sliced in half

450 g/1 lb leeks, washed and cut into 6 mm/¼ inch slices

juice of a lemon

1 tablespoon coriander chopped

olive oil

ground black pepper

Fry the leeks in the olive oil in a frying pan on a medium heat for 2-3 minutes, until beginning to soften. Add the scallops and fry until they start to colour and become soft. Add the lemon juice, ground black pepper and chopped coriander to the scallop juices, and heat through. Serve with good bread or new potatoes.

# RED, WHITE & GREEN SCALLOPS

*Serves 4*

This is a wonderfully fresh and colourful dish, and takes no time at all to prepare and cook. Asparagus makes it rather special, but another green vegetable such as fresh peas or French beans is just as good – perfect food for a summer's evening.

## INGREDIENTS

24 scallops, cleaned and sliced in half

225 g/8 oz cherry tomatoes

1 large onion roughly chopped

1 red pepper chopped finely

225 g/8 oz chopped asparagus, peas *or* French beans, already lightly cooked

olive oil

1 glass white wine

2 tablespoons chopped coriander or parsley

Gently fry the onion and the red pepper, and when they are just beginning to soften and colour add the tomatoes. As the tomato skins begin to split, press each one to allow some of the juice to escape. Add the scallops and cook gently for a minute, before adding the wine and asparagus. Cook until the scallops are soft, gently stir through the coriander or parsley.

Serve with rice flavoured by cooking with 2 quarters of a lemon in the water.

# SEA BASS WITH FRESH HERB BUTTER

*Serves 4*

Much of the bass on sale is farmed; fresh wild sea bass is caught in the waters of the South-west. It is at its best between June and February. Unfortunately it is expensive but it is worth buying once in a while, as it is a superb fish and best cooked simply.

## INGREDIENTS

4 fillets sea bass

50 g/2 oz butter softened

1 dessertspoon French parsley

1 dessertspoon chives

1 teaspoon thyme

$\frac{1}{2}$ glass white wine or dry sherry

olive oil

coarse sea salt and ground black pepper

Mix the herbs with the softened butter. Place the bass fillets in an ovenproof dish and smear with the butter mixture. Season to taste and pour the wine or sherry around the fish.

Place in a hot oven 230ºC/450ºF/gas mark 8 for 10 minutes. Watch the cooking time carefully – the fish should only be just done and the butter not burnt.

Serve with some extravagant vegetable such as asparagus or really fresh garden peas. Nothing could be finer.

# SEAFOOD WITH MUSTARD & CREAM

*Serves 4*

This recipe is a homage to Rick Stein who has done so much to promote fish and fish cookery over the years. It is based on his seafood thermidor, an early recipe much loved by those who went to his restaurant – although made simpler for this book.

The original recipe is in English Seafood Cookery (Penguin, 1988) by 'Richard' Stein!

## INGREDIENTS

450 g/1 lb assorted filleted white fish – it does not matter which fish except that there needs to be a variety of textures

4 scallops cut in half

110 g/4 oz cooked shelled prawns

110 g/4 oz button mushrooms halved

1 leek sliced thinly

butter

$\frac{1}{2}$ glass white wine

juice of $\frac{1}{2}$ lemon

275 ml/10 fl oz double cream mixed with

$\frac{1}{2}$ tablespoon English mustard powder

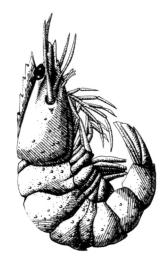

1 heaped tablespoon grated Parmesan

1 tablespoon parsley chopped

Place the leek, mushrooms, fish and scallops in a buttered ovenproof dish with the white wine and the lemon juice. Bake in a hot oven 230ºC/450ºF/gas mark 8 for 8 minutes and then drain off the liquid.

Add the prawns and then pour over the cream and the mustard mixture. Sprinkle the Parmesan across the top and return to the oven for a further 5 minutes until the fish is cooked and the cream bubbling. Decorate with the parsley before serving. New potatoes and spinach are excellent with this dish.

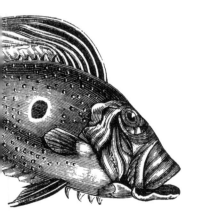
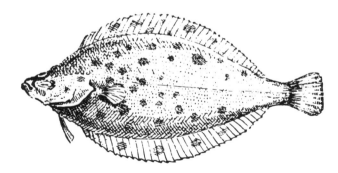

# MEGRIM SOLE WITH CLOTTED CREAM & CHIVES

*Serves 4*

Megrim is a sole which is caught a great deal in the West Country and is as delicious as lemon sole. Sadly it remains unappreciated by many and much of it is exported.

## INGREDIENTS

4 megrim sole filleted

110g/4oz clotted cream

2 tablespoons chopped chives

1oz butter

coarse sea salt and ground black pepper

¼ teaspoon paprika

Butter an ovenproof dish that will hold all 4 fish in one layer. Spread the clotted cream and the chives between the fillets of each fish. Dot the top of the fish with a little butter and the salt and pepper to taste.

Bake in a hot oven 230°C/450°F/gas mark 8 for 10 minutes. Dust with paprika to decorate, and serve.

Spinach and new potatoes go well with the megrim.

# TORBAY SOLE STUFFED WITH CRAB & PRAWNS

*Serves 4*

Torbay sole is lovely and yet is often shunned simply because it is less well known – in fact its name has been changed from witch sole in an effort to make it more popular. It tastes every bit as good as lemon sole and can be fatter with denser flesh.

## INGREDIENTS

4 small or 2 large Torbay soles filleted

20 prawns

225g/8 oz mixed crabmeat

225ml/8 fl oz double cream

juice of 2 lemons

2 tablespoons chives chopped

sea salt and ground black pepper to taste

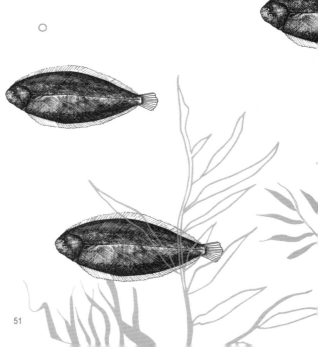

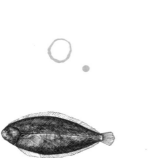

Cut the prawns in half and mix with the crabmeat, most of the chives and the double cream – this is the stuffing mixture. Pour a little of the lemon juice into an ovenproof dish. If the fillets are small, first lay down the bottom fillet, placing some stuffing on top and then covering with the other fillet. If they are large soles, the fillets will need to be cut lengthways before stuffing them in the same manner.

Add sea salt and ground black pepper to taste and cover with the remainder of the lemon juice – you will have to use your judgement: if the lemons are large you may not need to use all the juice.

Place in a hot oven 230°C/450°F/gas mark 8 for 15-20 minutes depending on the thickness of the sole – check after 15 to be on the safe side. Decorate with the remainder of the chives.

# SQUID WITH GARLIC, CORIANDER & OLIVES

*Serves 4*

Squid (and octopus) look somewhat scary to prepare but fishmongers are only too willing to do the tricky work for you. It is fished all the year but is best in winter. While it is much more popular than it used to be, much of the catch is still exported. This is a very quick and simple dish which has a flavour full of the sunny south.

## INGREDIENTS

350g/12oz squid sliced

1 medium onion finely chopped

2 cloves garlic chopped

2 tablespoons coriander chopped

12 green olives pitted and roughly chopped

2 tablespoons sherry or white wine

olive oil

Put a little olive oil in a frying pan and add the onion and garlic, cooking until soft. Add the squid and fry quickly for 2 minutes over a hot flame, turning constantly. Add the olives and the coriander and white wine. Mix together over the flame and serve straight away with plain boiled rice decorated with 1 tablespoon of pine nuts.

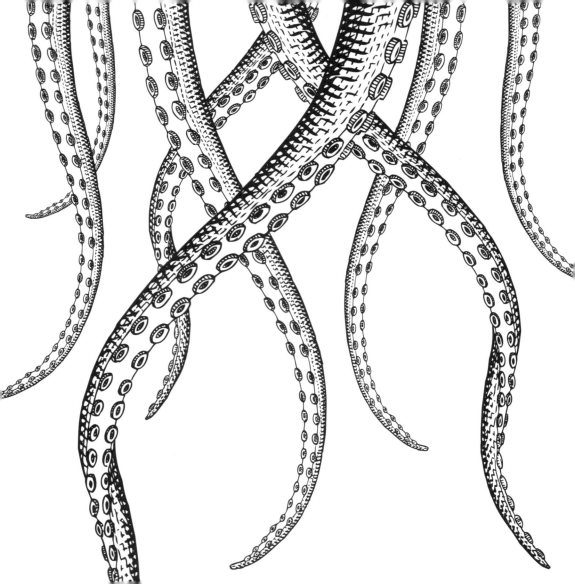

# HOT SQUID SALAD

Hot salads are always fun to do – they are instant food with the delight of the hot ingredients and dressing.

## INGREDIENTS

350 g/12 oz squid roughly sliced

4 spring onions

225 g/8 oz tomatoes cut into chunks

10 cm/4 inch piece of cucumber cut into chunks

1 cabbage lettuce or assorted salad leaves

12 black olives pitted

2 tablespoons assorted chopped herbs

12 seedless grapes cut in half

4 tablespoons olive oil

1 tablespoon white wine vinegar

coarse sea salt and ground black pepper to taste

Firstly assemble the salad in a large bowl. Place some of the olive oil in a frying pan and over a high heat fry the octopus for 2 minutes. Add the rest of the olive oil and warm it through, then add the wine vinegar – be careful: it will hiss and steam and make your eyes water!

Pour the squid and dressing over the salad, add salt and ground black pepper to taste, and mix the salad thoroughly so that the lettuce begins to wilt and all the ingredients are thoroughly mixed. Serve immediately with warm French bread.

# TUNA AND CORIANDER, LEMON & WHITE WINE

*Serves 4*

Tuna is caught 3-4 weeks a year out of Newlyn but is always readily available on supermarket fish stalls. Although expensive, tuna is very filling, so the portions can be quite small. It is straightforward to cook and versatile – it looks like pale meat and can be treated very like fillet steak. It is important not to overcook it.

## INGREDIENTS

4 x 75g/3oz slices of tuna not more than 12mm/$\frac{1}{2}$ inch thick

juice of 1 lemon

$\frac{1}{2}$ glass white wine

olive oil

2 tablespoons chopped coriander

2 cloves garlic chopped

Cover the base of an ovenproof dish with a little olive oil, place the tuna slices in the dish and cover with the rest of the ingredients. Bake in a hot oven 230ºC/450ºF/gas mark 8 for 10-15 minutes and serve with new potatoes and courgettes.

# TUNA STEW

*Serves 4*

This is a reminder of holidays in sunnier climates – tuna is readily available in Spain, Portugal and Southern France, and because of its meat-like qualities lends itself to being stewed with Mediterranean vegetables. The French parsley is used here because of the hint of celery in the chopped stalks.

## INGREDIENTS

350g/12oz tuna cut into large chunks

1 medium onion roughly chopped

½ red pepper roughly chopped

½ green pepper roughly chopped

1 medium courgette roughly chopped

1 x 400g/14oz tin chopped tomatoes

2 teaspoons tomato purée

¼ teaspoon dried oregano

olive oil

coarse sea salt and ground black pepper to taste

1 tablespoon chopped French parsley

Fry all the vegetables in a little olive oil in an ovenproof casserole over a medium heat. When they are beginning to soften add the tomato purée, tinned tomatoes, oregano, salt and pepper to taste, and lastly the tuna. Mix gently together and place in a medium oven 180ºC/350ºF/gas mark 4 for about 30 minutes or until the vegetables and tuna are cooked through. Sprinkle the chopped parsley on top and serve with plain boiled rice or couscous.

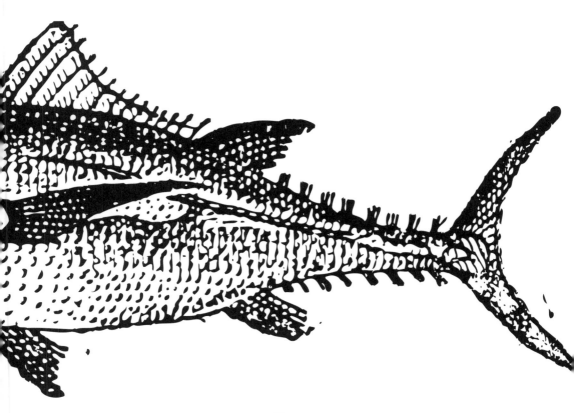

# GREEK HADDOCK

*Serves 4*

A dish that many will have had on holiday in the Mediterranean. Haddock or any other white fish can be used.

## INGREDIENTS

4 x 150-175g/5-6oz pieces of haddock fillet

olive oil

1 glass white wine

1 lemon squeezed

1 onion chopped

2 cloves garlic chopped

1 tablespoon chopped parsley

2 green peppers chopped

4 large tomatoes roughly chopped

4 medium potatoes roughly sliced

coarse sea salt and ground black pepper to taste

Lightly oil an oven-proof dish. Place the potatoes in it and bake in the oven until lightly browned and nearly cooked. Fry the onion, garlic and peppers in olive oil until nearly soft, add the tomatoes, the lemon juice, wine, parsley, salt and pepper to taste and simmer for 5 minutes until nearly cooked. Place the haddock fillets on top of the nearly cooked potatoes and cover with the vegetable mixture. Add a little more liquid if it seems dry. Cook for 20 minutes, medium oven 180ºC/350ºF/gas mark 4 or until the fish is cooked.

# NOTES

# NOTES